Securing the Wireless Frontier

How Blockchain Tech Enhances IoT Security

Table of Contents

Chapter 1. Introduction

As our digital lives expand into a wireless frontier dominated by the Internet of Things (IoT), the threats associated with data security also intensify. The solution could lie within an unconventional ally, Blockchain technology. Our comprehensive Special Report, "Securing the Wireless Frontier: How Blockchain Tech Enhances IoT Security," demystifies the intricate relationship between these two transformative technologies in a manner digestible for all readers. By the end of this report, you will grasp why and how Blockchain technology plays a pivotal role in fortifying IoT security, nullifying potential breaches and ensuring the sanctity of our digital existence. Armed with this knowledge, you'll have the confidence to navigate this vast cybernetic landscape knowing your devices and data are protected by a resilient shield of cryptographic might.

Chapter 2. Understanding the Basics: IoT and Blockchain

Before we immerse ourselves in the interaction between Blockchain and IoT, we must firstly understand these concepts individually. This chapter will take you on a journey through the fundamental aspects of both IoT and Blockchain, meanwhile laying down a solid foundation for our discussion of their synergies.

2.1. Definition and Overview of IoT

IoT, an acronym for the Internet of Things, refers to the network of billions of physical devices globally that connect and exchange data over the internet. It's not merely about smart devices or home automation, albeit they constitute a portion of it. IoT extends its bounds to smart cities, wearable health monitors, connected vehicles, and more.

This rapid interconnection and data exchange burgeons several opportunities including but not limited to, enhanced efficiency, improved decision making and resource optimization. Industrial applications of IoT often call it Industrial Internet of Things (IIoT), which leverage data to make operations efficient and innovate new products. The interoperability and constant connectivity of these devices across a network result in a constant generation and sharing of data.

While these numerous advantages of IoT revolutionize various sectors, they also pose significant security risks. The increased frequency of data sharing opens numerous avenues for potential data breaches, unauthorized access, and privacy intrusion. Hence, securing this network of devices becomes paramount.

2.2. Definition and Overview of Blockchain

The term "Blockchain" denotes a suitable list or sequence of records, known as blocks, linked via cryptography. Introduced primarily as a public transaction ledger for the cryptocurrency Bitcoin, Blockchain has applications extending far beyond the realm of digital currencies.

One of the main features of Blockchain technology includes its decentralized and distributed nature. It does not rely on a central authority. Instead, it keeps multiple ledger copies across computers around the world, known as nodes. This distributed network forms a chain of data blocks, each containing information and the cryptographic hash of the previous block.

The decentralized nature of Blockchain imparts it with the dual advantages of transparency and security. The lack of a single point of failure, coupled with the cryptographic linkage of blocks, makes it highly secure against data tampering. Meanwhile, an auditable trail of transactions ensures transparency of operations and data authenticity.

While Blockchain was initially associated with monetary transactions, today it has manifold applications like smart contracts, decentralized applications (dApps), and supply chain tracking, thus increasing its appeal as a secure data recording technology.

2.3. The Confluence of IoT and Blockchain: A Need Arises

The vast amount of data generated by IoT devices and applications requires a secure, efficient, decentralized, and scalable solution for its storage and management. Enter Blockchain. As we have seen, this technology bears inherent features suitable for addressing the security, privacy, and trust issues associated with IoT.

Some key challenges that IoT faces, such as data threats, lack of transparency, single points of failure, and difficulties in managing and processing vast quantities of data, coincide with the areas where Blockchain technology shines. This realization expands the horizons of both Blockchain and IoT while allowing them to compensate for each other's limitations.

That brings us to the importance of the relationship between Blockchain and IoT in facilitating secure data transmission and management.

2.4. Compatible Features of IoT and Blockchain

Several features of Blockchain and IoT align perfectly, resulting in an ideal combination to address security issues. Blockchain's inherent properties, such as decentralization, immutability, and transparency gel well, with IoT's interconnectivity, and edge computing capabilities.

The decentralized structure of Blockchain can eliminate the need for a central authority in IoT networks. Consequently, this brings forth a trustless environment where devices can interact and transact without relying on intermediaries. Furthermore, Blockchain's ability to create immutable records ensures an auditable trail of data, thereby enhancing transparency and security. This immutable log of data can, in turn, help in integrity assurance of IoT data, thus safeguarding against potential data tampering.

Blockchain's smart contract functionality can automate processes in an IoT network, thereby reducing costs and enhancing efficiency. Besides, IoT's edge computing capabilities, when combined with Blockchain, can enhance the scalability and speed of data processing, thus making the joint system more efficient.

Despite these promising facets, we also need to consider the limitations and obstacles in integrating Blockchain with IoT.

2.5. Challenges in Integrating IoT and Blockchain

The integration of Blockchain and IoT presents exciting possibilities, but it's not without its set of challenges. Scalability, energy consumption, and technological maturity are some significant issues to be addressed.

Blockchain's current transaction speed or throughput is comparatively slower due to its size and growth, which can be an impediment for IoT applications that require real-time data processing. Moreover, Blockchain's power-hungry consensus mechanisms, such as Proof of Work (PoW), can result in increased energy consumption, which isn't efficient or sustainable in the long-run.

The complexity of Blockchain technology not only complicates its understanding and adoption but also the development of standards and interoperability protocols for its application in IoT. Given the wide range of IoT devices, developing universal standards and protocols is indeed a challenge.

Despite these hurdles, the potential benefits make the integration worthwhile, necessitating continued research, planning, and development to bring this idea to fruition.

By understanding both IoT and Blockchain individually, as well as the promise and challenges of their integration, we set the ground for our following exploration where we analyze how Blockchain enhances IoT security and reliability. While one technology signifies connection, the other ensures security – together creating an innovative landscape full of potential. As we venture further, we will delve deeper into specifics of this intersection of Blockchain with IoT, illuminating the uncharted paths of digital security.

Chapter 3. Unfolding Security Concerns in The IoT Landscape

The evolution of IoT, while remarkable in its breadth, carries emerging security challenges. In order to understand the potential role blockchain can play in securing this landscape, we must first unpack the various concerns that surround IoT security.

3.1. Understanding IoT and its Vulnerabilities

IoT, shorthand for the Internet of Things, denotes an interconnected network of physical devices, vehicles, home appliances, and other items embedded with sensors, software, and network connectivity. These capabilities allows these objects to gather and exchange data, creating opportunities for more direct integration between the digital world and the physical one.

The expansive nature of these networks, however, makes them a prime target for numerous security threats. Security is often an afterthought during the development of IoT devices, which prioritizes functionality and ease of use over this crucial aspect. This neglect of security considerations leads to vulnerabilities that adversaries can exploit to gain unauthorized access, disrupt service, or steal sensitive data.

3.2. Common Security Concerns for IoT devices

The security concerns related to IoT devices can be categorized under a few main threats:

1. Data Privacy: IoT devices constantly collect, store, and transmit data, some of which can be highly sensitive. In the wrong hands, this data can be used for malicious purposes like identity theft or financial fraud.

2. Unauthorized Access: Weak security protocols may allow potential attackers to gain control over IoT devices. They could then misuse these devices, causing harm or disruption to the users or networks in question.

3. Device and System Disruptions: IoT devices are often integral to the operation of larger systems, be it an automated home, a manufacturing line, or a city's infrastructure. Cyber attacks that disrupt the operation of these devices can lead to significant consequences.

4. Eavesdropping: IoT devices such as smart speakers, video cameras, and other monitoring devices could be manipulated to spy on users and collect sensitive information.

3.3. IoT Security and Data In Transit

One of the key imperatives for IoT devices is to ensure the secure transmission of data, often termed as "data in transit". Given the remote nature of these devices - which may include being located in public areas or across broad geographic spans - securing the data these devices communicate is a non-trivial challenge.

Data in transit is susceptible to various attacks, including 'man-in-the-middle' attack, where intruders intercept and potentially alter the data being transmitted. The traditional methods of securing data in transit, such as encryption, can be insufficient without a robust way to verify the trustworthiness of devices on each endpoint.

3.4. Insights from Real-world Security Breaches

Experiences from past security breaches provide us insights into how tangible these threats could be. Several high-profile incidents have demonstrated the significant potential for harm:

1. The Mirai botnet, created in 2016, took control of poorly protected IoT devices and directed them in one of the largest distributed denial-of-service (DDoS) attacks on record.

2. The Stuxnet worm targeted industrial control systems, leading to significant damage to Iran's nuclear program.

3. Smart home hacks have invaded the privacy of individuals, with attackers gaining access to cameras, smart locks, and other connected devices.

Each of these incidents underscores the serious potential for security breaches in the IoT landscape moving forwards.

3.5. The Current State of IoT Security Measures

Despite the known security threats, IoT security measures in many devices currently in use are far from adequate. Many IoT devices lack basic security features such as strong authentication and encryption. This lax attitude towards security, often due to the rush to get products to market, the constraint of device resources, or the lack of regulation, has resulted in an environment where securing IoT devices is often more reactive than proactive.

Additionally, IoT devices may be in operation for many years, making them susceptible to new threats that emerge after their deployment. This lack of post-deployment updates has been identified as a significant threat to the long-term security of IoT devices.

The examination of these concerns surrounding IoT security sets the stage for the introduction of a crypto-secured toolkit for navigating this new frontier – Blockchain. As we will explore in the following chapters, blockchain technology may hold the key to strengthen the defenses of the IoT landscape against the vulnerabilities exposed here. If properly implemented, this technology could provide a robust shield for our digital lives in the proliferating world of IoT.

Chapter 4. Blockchain 101: A Comprehensive Overview

To understand how Blockchain can augment IoT security, we first need to comprehend how Blockchain functions fundamentally. Blockchain is more than just a technology backing the world of cryptocurrencies; it is a pivotal tool for secure data sharing.

Blockchain, fundamentally, is a distributed, decentralized, and tamper-proof ledger that chronicles a data exchange among a group of individuals without the need for an intermediary. Each exchange represents a block, and each block becomes an unalterable part of the ledger, a chain, hence the term 'Blockchain.'

4.1. Understanding Decentralization

Decentralization is a foundational aspect of Blockchain. In traditional systems, a single entity (like banks) holds authority and maintains data. Here, the integrity of data hangs in balance with this centralized authority's integrity, making the system prone to single-point failures or cyber-attacks.

In contrast, Blockchain's decentralized approach means that the authority is spread across the network nodes. Each node in the network carries a copy of the entire ledger, and all nodes must approve a new block before it becomes part of the chain. This decentralized approach increases the system's robustness as compromising one node won't affect the ledger's integrity. The replicative nature of the ledger across all nodes makes it virtually impossible for a malicious attack to alter existing blocks successfully.

4.2. The Principle of Transparency and Anonymity

Blockchain operates on transparency and anonymity principles. While all transactions are visible to all network participants, users remain anonymous with unique online addresses. The transparency feature assists in maintaining transactional accountability and immutability. On the other hand, anonymity preserves privacy while ensuring non-repudiation of transactions. Thus, the system provides a subtle blend of accountability, immutability, and privacy.

4.3. Understanding Cryptographic Security

Blockchain's security lies in its use of advanced cryptography. Each block contains a cryptographic hash, a unique digital fingerprint of the preceding block, data of the current block, and its unique hash. This cryptographic connection between blocks ensures that, if an attacker modifies a single block, it would pose discrepancies in the subsequent blocks.

The underlying cryptographic hash function translates data into a unique hash value, such that any minor change in the data radically changes the hash value. This feature, combined with the requirement of network consensus, fortifies the Blockchain against tampering.

4.4. The Role of Consensus

Consensus algorithms play an essential role in Blockchain technology. They validate the authenticity of transactions and blocks. Two prevalent consensus mechanisms in Blockchain are Proof of Work (PoW) and Proof of Stake (PoS).

PoW necessitates miners to solve computationally intensive puzzles; the first to solve gets to add the new block. However, the power-intensive nature of PoW has brought PoS into the limelight.

PoS vests the power to add new blocks based on the user's stake or the number of coins they hold and are willing to 'stake' as collateral. The staked cryptocurrencies act as a deterrent against malicious activities. Thus, consensus mechanisms deter inappropriate behavior while securing the network.

4.5. Types of Blockchain Networks

Blockchain networks come in various types, primarily Public, Private and Consortium Blockchains.

Public Blockchains, like Bitcoin and Ethereum, are entirely open, allowing anyone to participate and transact. Private Blockchains, on the other hand, restrict participation rights and only predefined entities can validate transactions. Consortium Blockchain (or Federated Blockchain) is a partially private Blockchain where multiple organizations control the system collectively.

Each type suits different use cases, with Public blockchain offering maximum decentralization and transparency suitable for cryptocurrencies, Private blockchains suitable for enterprises prioritizing control and privacy, and Consortium blockchains suitable for collaborative business models.

4.6. Smart Contracts: The Game Changer

Smart Contracts, programmable contracts that self-execute upon meeting set criteria, are a critical Blockchain addition enhancing its universal applicability. Parties in an agreement can directly write contracts into lines of code. The programmed smart contract autonomously verifies fulfillment, ensuring contractual obligations are automated, accurate, and transparent, marking an evolutionary jump in contract enforcement.

By understanding the underpinnings of Blockchain technology, its cryptographic security, consensus mechanisms, types, and the power of smart contracts, one can see how Blockchain is poised as a powerful tool. As the subsequent chapters will demonstrate, the principles that secure Blockchain also make it a strong ally in fortifying IoT security.

Chapter 5. Demystifying How Blockchain Works in IoT Security

Integration of Blockchain technology to the Internet of Things (IoT) realm promises unprecedented levels of data security. There's a myriad of potential applications, yet the complex interworking of these two phenomena remains an enigma to many. Together, we'll explore the intricacies of these seemingly complex relationships to give you in-depth understanding and mastery of the nexus between Blockchain and IoT security.

5.1. The Origin of Blockchain and its Evolution

Blockchain, at its core, is a decentralized and distributed ledger technology. It originated as the underlying operational framework for Bitcoin, the infamous cryptocurrency engineered by the pseudonymous Satoshi Nakamoto in 2008. Unlike conventional databases, which operate on a central server, blockchain distributes its transactions across numerous personal computers worldwide, creating a system that is inherently decentralized.

Throughout its existence, blockchain has repeatedly proven its capability to adequately secure digital transactions. Its features such as immutability, transparency, and decentralization, have earned it a coveted spot in many integrations beyond cryptocurrency, one of which is securing IoT networks.

5.2. Understanding Blockchain

By definition, a blockchain is a growing list of records (blocks), linked using cryptography where each block contains a cryptographic hash of the previous block, a timestamp, and transaction data. The hallmark of this technology is its intentionally designed resistance to data modification.

Blockchain employs a consensus protocol to validate transactions, which involves multiple network nodes agreeing on the blockchain state. The result is an environment where no single node can unilaterally update the blockchain, therefore ensuring the integrity and immutability of data.

Additional security comes from the cryptographic techniques. For instance, if a cybercriminal attempts to alter any transaction, it'd require changing all preceding blocks due to the interlinked nature of blocks, which in practicality is next to impossible due to high computational requirements and the need to control more than 50% of network nodes – a feat immensely difficult to achieve.

5.3. Blockchain and IoT: A Natural Symbiosis

The Internet of Things comprises devices interconnected over the internet, ranging from home appliances to industrial machinery. These devices generate and communicate vast datasets, inevitably raising concerns about data security and privacy.

Despite the unique challenges presented by IoT, blockchain technology brings forth a tailored solution. Its decentralized, transparent, and immutable nature provides an excellent platform to safeguard data integrity while its automated smart contracts enable seamless device communication and interaction.

5.4. Securing IoT with Blockchain

Traditional centralized IoT networks have inherent vulnerabilities - they serve as tempting targets for cyberattackers. Once an attacker gains control over the central server, they could manipulate IoT devices at will. But by using blockchain as a decentralized network, the risk is dispersed. Each IoT device operates as an independent blockchain node, meaning a potential attacker needs to compromise an impossible number of devices to cause havoc.

Blockchain also allows for the creation, verification, and enforcement of smart contracts – self-executing applications under specified conditions. In an IoT context, smart contracts enable devices to make autonomous decisions without needing human intervention.

5.5. Privacy Protection and Anonymity

A critical aspect of blockchain technology is its ability to ensure anonymity while ensuring participants' accountability. This attribute bodes well with the inherently privacy-invasive IoT devices since it can provide robust privacy protection.

Each IoT device with its blockchain identity is anonymous but verifiable on the blockchain network. Transactions are traceable and transparent but without revealing the identity linked to the IoT device. This mechanism maintains privacy without affecting system integrity, providing a balance between transparency and privacy.

5.6. Pitching Challenges for Cyberattackers

Blockchain establishes a daunting barrier for potential cyberattackers. Since the IoT device identities on the network are recorded on blockchain's immutable, transparent ledger, any illegitimate attempt to manipulate IoT devices becomes instantly noticeable. An attacker would need to gain control over 51% of the network's nodes, which is a considerably challenging feat given the computational demand and resources required.

5.7. Future Directions

As more industries incorporate IoT devices and the scale of these networks continues to grow, so too will the complexities of data security. The integration of blockchain with IoT offers promising potential to comprehensively address these challenges. By effectively leveraging blockchain's distinct features, we can create a secure, efficient, and reliable IoT landscape.

To conclude, by decrypting the functioning of blockchain in IoT security, we shed light on the resiliency and robustness of these converging technologies, making it evident how, unlike the stereotypical perception, blockchain serves as a boon, far exceeding cryptocurrencies' periphery. A series of characteristics, including decentralized control, immutability, transparency, and automatic execution of smart contracts, makes it adaptable to IoT, ultimately fortifying our wireless frontier.

Chapter 6. Common Threats: IoT Vulnerabilities Addressed by Blockchain

Our digital world is continually evolving, and with it, the Internet of Things (IoT) landscape experiences frequent changes. Unfortunately, these alterations occasionally result in an array of threats and vulnerabilities that compromise the security of our interconnected devices. However, many of these vulnerabilities can be addressed by blockchain technology—a revolutionary system that offers robust security measures unparalleled in today's digital era.

6.1. IoT Vulnerabilities

When we delve into the realm of IoT, it's paramount to understand the vulnerabilities that plague this burgeoning digital sector. IoT devices often handle a vast array of sensitive information, from personal details to corporate secrets and top-tier government data. This information, if mishandled or stolen, can lead to severe consequences ranging from an individual's identity theft to large-scale national security breaches.

Many of these IoT devices lack the necessary protections needed to shield this sensitive data effectively. These vulnerabilities primarily arise from the following areas:

1. **Default Passwords and Weak Security Settings:** Many IoT devices come outfitted with easily Google-able default passwords—open invitations to malicious actors looking to gain unauthorized access. Additionally, these devices often lack the rigorous security settings synonymous with computer systems or mobile apps, leaving them even more exposed.

2. **Lack of Data Encryption:** Much of the data transferred between devices in the IoT framework is sent "in the clear," meaning it isn't encrypted. This lack of encryption allows potential attackers to intercept data without much difficulty.

3. **Insecure Networks and Lack of Update Mechanisms:** IoT devices, more often than not, are linked to insecure networks with little-to-no protection against cyber threats. The situation worsens when considering these networks are usually devoid of automatic update mechanisms—paving a clear pathway for exploitation by hackers capitalizing on vulnerabilities unearthed after the devices come into circulation.

6.2. How Blockchain Addresses IoT Vulnerabilities

Blockchain, in essence, is a decentralized ledger of transactions distributed over a vast network of computers. By virtue of its structure, blockchain offers multiple strengths that effectively address IoT vulnerabilities.

Secured Identity Verification: Blockchain uses cryptographic algorithms for identity verification. This method ensures each IoT device on a network is authenticated and the data transmitted is executed by registered devices alone. This authentication eliminates concerns about pseudo-devices entering the network, thereby providing a resilient shield against unauthorized access.

Enhanced Data Integrity: With data breaches becoming increasingly common, maintaining data integrity is crucial. Blockchain technology not only ensures that data is recorded correctly but also guarantees it has not been tampered with—making manipulations virtually impossible due to the immutability aspect of blockchain.

Data Encryption: Blockchain employs advanced cryptographic techniques that make the data transferred over networks encrypted by default. This encryption ensures that even if an attacker intercepts the data, they cannot comprehend it without the corresponding decryption key, ensuring the preservation of data safety.

Secure, Automated Updates: A blockchain-based framework facilitates the secure, automatic updating of devices within the IoT landscape. Because the blockchain system conducts updates in a distributed, ledger-based manner, it ensures that all devices within the network receive updates simultaneously—nipping potential exploitation of outdated systems in the bud.

6.3. Operational Enhancement and Business Benefits

Blockchain's innate features not only address IoT vulnerabilities but also streamline operations and accrue several business benefits to stakeholders:

Reduced Costs: A blockchain-based IoT framework eliminates intermediaries, leading to automated transactions that significantly reduce operational costs.

Improved Transparency: The distributed nature of blockchain ensures complete transparency, as every transaction is recorded and visible to all the network participants.

Increased Efficiency: Transactions executed on blockchain are swift and liberated from manual errors, greatly improving efficiency.

In conclusion, as the IoT landscape continues to expand and evolve, security threats keep pace. However, blockchain technology serves as the antidote to many of these security risks, effectively addressing the vulnerabilities inherent in IoT devices. Its unique combination of expansive features, such as secured identity verification, enhanced data integrity, data encryption, and secure automatic updates, bestows an unprecedented level of security to the IoT framework. With the additional advantages of reduced costs, improved transparency, and increased efficiency, the alliance of blockchain and IoT promises to fortify the digital landscape.

Chapter 7. Blockchain-IoT Interplay: Real-world Case Studies

The application of Blockchain technology to improve Internet of Things (IoT) security is not just theoretical; it has already found implementation across various spheres of activity. From logistics and healthcare to autonomous vehicles and smart cities, these instances of real-world employments illustrate how Blockchain can enhance IoT security.

7.1. Logistical Efficiency with Blockchain

The logistics industry relies heavily on IoT devices for tracking shipments and goods. Traditional approaches, however, expose this industry to significant security challenges. This was evident in the 2017 NotPetya ransomware attack that affected Maersk, causing a loss of about $300M. Blockchain technology offers a solution to these issues.

For instance, IBM and Maersk launched TradeLens, a Blockchain-based platform for digital supply chain management, post the NotPetya incident. The platform brought transparency, data sharing with tamper-evident logs and greater efficiency through smart contracts execution. A test run involved shipping a container from Korea to the Netherlands, wherein the traditional paper-intensive process involving multiple hand-offs was successfully replaced by an immutable distributed ledger.

7.2. Blockchain in Healthcare Industry

Security of data and ensuring its proper utilization is critical in the healthcare industry, and IoT devices are integral to managing this data. The integration of Blockchain with IoT can revolutionize the scenario.

MediLedger, a collaborative project involving some of the biggest pharmaceutical companies, illustrates this. It uses a private, permissioned Blockchain network for tracing the provenance of drugs, securing data against tampering. IoT devices facilitate temperature regulation and tracking, which, combined with the Blockchain, ensure trustable data records.

Similarly, MIT's MedRec platform uses Ethereum Blockchain to manage permissions to health records, making records interoperable, easy to access for patients and doctors, and secure.

7.3. Autonomous Vehicles and Blockchain

Autonomous vehicles, powered by numerous IoT devices, are prone to cyber threats. Data tampering can have catastrophic consequences on the road. Blockchain implementation in autonomous cars can prevent these security challenges.

Car Vertical, a car history registry, uses a Blockchain-based system, ensuring data integrity and preventing odometer fraud. In the same vein, MOBI (The Mobility Open Blockchain Initiative) integrates Blockchain with IoT devices in vehicles. It validates the information from each vehicle, making data manipulation for malicious purposes practically impossible.

7.4. Smart Cities Rely on Blockchain

The implementation of Blockchain in smart city initiatives ensures security, privacy, and reliability of the data involved. A smart city integrates multiple IoT devices to facilitate efficient urban living, but a security breach could lead to chaos.

In Dubai, Blockchain technology is at the core of its smart city initiative. From land registry, business registration to even citizen identity verification, it all happens on a Blockchain, with data security and integrity ensured by design.

Similarly, in Moscow, the Active Citizen platform leverages Ethereum Blockchain to record citizens' votes on various city issues, making the process transparent and the votes immune to tampering.

7.5. Conclusion

The adoption of Blockchain technology in IoT is not only a suitable solution to address data security concerns but also a catalyst to transform and improve processes in various industries. By understanding the value and advantages Blockchain technology brings, future advancements can be geared towards evolving a safer, efficient, and trustworthy IoT ecosystem. Mindful adoption of the technology will undoubtedly secure the wireless frontier aiding humankind in marching towards a digital future with safety and assurance. The real-world case studies offer a glimpse into this promising future and inspire us on how Blockchain's immutable, decentralized nature can seamlessly merge with IoT for a safer, more secure digital world.

Chapter 8. Assessment of Present IoT-Blockchain Solutions

The emergence of IoT technology has revolutionized the way we perceive and interact with the world around us. Everyday objects have become channels of data transmission, creating an intricately woven network of interconnected devices. Nevertheless, the expanding web of these smart devices creates numerous openings for malign forces to exploit. This has put the spotlight on data security and, in this regard, blockchain technology has proven to be a potent ally.

Despite the promise, current IoT-Blockchain solutions bear their share of vulnerabilities along with benefits. To fully comprehend the impact of blockchain tech on IoT security, this assessment will delve extensively into current solutions, examining their strengths and weaknesses, and exploring implications for the future.

8.1. IoT-Blockchain Security Informatics

The first aspect that requires examination involves understanding the informational aspects of security in the IoT-Blockchain ecosystem. Blockchain's inherent encryption methodology plays an essential role in bolstering IoT security. By linking blocks of data cryptographically, blockchain forms an almost unassailable fortress against data breaches.

Simultaneously, blockchain's decentralized nature frees IoT networks from the vulnerabilities of centralized servers. In doing so, it not only increases the resilience of these smart networks against potential attacks but also enhances the integrity of the data being transmitted.

However, these benefits carry potential challenges. The encryption techniques utilized by blockchain can sometimes result in increased latencies, hampering the real-time responses of IoT devices. Furthermore, while decentralization improves security, it could also make the identification and resolution of security breaches more complicated due to the need for consensus.

8.2. Hardware and Software Considerations

Blockchain serves as an excellent method to secure data on the transmission side. However, the physical components of the IoT network - the devices themselves - could potentially serve as weak points. Modern IoT devices are usually fitted with lightweight software due to their limited processing capabilities.

While most current IoT-Blockchain solutions emphasize software security, they tend to neglect the physical aspects. For example, an attacker could potentially tamper with a device to alter its data before it even reaches the blockchain-secured network. Hence, the physical security of IoT devices is an area needing significant enhancement.

On the software side, protocols need to be optimized to meet the processing limitations of IoT devices. Since blockchain can be computationally intensive, this could pose substantial challenges to these solutions. Prioritizing lightweight consensus algorithms could be one way to approach this problem, but further innovation is required in this domain.

8.3. Scalability and Efficiency

As the IoT landscape expands, the strain on the blockchain network to accommodate the myriad of connected devices will increase. Scalability is a recognized issue within blockchain networks, with solutions like 'sharding' already under exploration to address this. However, these solutions are far from perfected and may take time to be effectively implemented on a large scale.

Moreover, the power consumed by blockchain processes remains a significant concern. With the carbon footprints of bitcoin mining making headlines, the efficiency of IoT-Blockchain solutions needs to be addressed. Innovative mechanisms to reduce the power consumption of these networks will need to be introduced to make these solutions sustainable for an IoT-dominated future.

8.4. Regulatory and Standardization Issues

Across the globe, the regulatory landscape for both IoT and blockchain is still in flux. This potpourri of differing rules and regulations can create implementation headaches. Additionally, standardization is still in its infancy. Without universal protocols or standards for IoT-Blockchain implementations, interoperability remains a challenge.

8.5. Conclusion

From this detailed examination of current IoT-Blockchain solutions, it is clear that while the fusion of these two technologies promises enhanced security, there are significant challenges ahead. As we move forward, overcoming these hurdles is crucial for the optimization of both blockchain and IoT, while ensuring the integrity and safety of our data in the wireless frontier.

Chapter 9. Blueprint for a Secure IoT Network: Leveraging Blockchain

The blueprint for a secure Internet of Things (IoT) network leveraging blockchain rests on the pillars of the blockchain's structure and mechanism itself. By deciphering its core components: Decentralization, Immutability, and Transparency, we can design an IoT ecosystem secure from its foundation to its myriad endpoints.

9.1. Decentralization: A Fundamental Paradigm Shift

Decentralization, one of the pillars of blockchain, offers a new way to distribute authority and control within an IoT network. Instead of a centrally controlled system, where decision-making and data storage occur in one central location, control within a blockchain ecosystem is distributed across a network of peers.

This peer-to-peer, non-hierarchical structure empowers each node (an IoT device in this context) to participate directly in the network. Each node has equal voting rights and constantly cross-verifies transactions against a consensus protocol. This systemic validation ensures absolute correctness of records, and if a single node comes under attack, the sanctity of the overall network remains unobliterated.

Rather than investing resources into securing a central point of failure (a practice in centralized systems), the focus of blockchain shifts to fortifying each node. This makes the network vastly more resilient against external threats. By preventing the traffic concentration to a single point, decentralization also contributes to smoother network operations and significantly reduced latency.

9.2. Immutability: Ensuring Data Integrity and Non-repudiation

Blockchain ensures that once a transaction is recorded, it is permanent. Storing transaction records in blocks and adding them sequentially to a chain of previous records ensures a tamper-proof environment. This inherent element of unalterability or immutability provides a robust shield to IoT devices against data manipulation.

Given that each record is mathematically related to its predecessor and successor, altering a single record will require changes to all subsequent blocks at the same time, a feat practically impossible given the consensus mechanism of the distributed network.

Furthermore, blockchain's cryptographic signatures also provide non-repudiation. Each transaction is linked to a specific key, ensuring that it is validated by the entity it originated from. In IoT's context, this translates to authorized devices making valid communication, addressing issues of device spoofing and unauthorized access.

9.3. Transparency: Promulgating Trust between Unknown Entities

Blockchain leverages transparency to build trust among nodes (IoT devices). Every validated transaction is visible to all participants of the network, making it easier to trace and verify transactions. While the contents may be visible, the identities of the parties involved are obfuscated and represented by their public keys.

In an IoT network, transparency helps account for the data generated by each device and the transactions they participate in. This holistic visibility reduces the shadowy corners where potential security breaches could lurk.

9.4. Smart Contracts: Self-executing Protocols Enhancing IoT Security

Smart contracts are programmable scripts that execute automatically when predefined conditions are met. These self-enforcing contracts can help automate various processes within the IoT network, reducing manual interference and the associated risks.

Smart contracts can regulate device permissions, validate the integrity of the data shared within the IoT system, and enforce obligation fulfillment between devices without a third-party intermediary. In case of compliance failure, the smart contract can execute countermeasures, thereby enhancing the robustness of the network.

9.5. Integration Challenges and Solutions

Despite its noticeable benefits, integrating blockchain technology with IoT doesn't imply the absence of challenges. Primary hurdles include integration complexity, consensus mechanism selection, and ensuring privacy.

1. **Integration Complexity**: Given the technological immaturity and lack of standardized protocols for blockchain's interoperation with IoT, integration complexity stands as a significant hurdle. Promoting collaboration between blockchain developers and IoT manufacturers, encouraging standards development, and fostering an open-source ecosystem are some ways to mitigate this challenge.

2. **Consensus Mechanism Selection**: Choosing the correct

consensus mechanism that aligns with the IoT network requirements is paramount. Depending on the application, a trade-off between security, scalability, and speed needs to be examined. Research into novel consensus algorithms tailored for IoT applications could provide a solution.

3. **Ensuring Privacy**: Balancing transparency with privacy is critical. Regulatory measures need to be devised that protect user data privacy while maintaining the benefits of a transparent, distributed ledger.

By tackling these challenges pragmatically, the fusion of blockchain technology and IoT can indeed serve as a powerful tool to secure the wireless frontier, guaranteeing the safety of our devices, the integrity of our data, and fortifying the bulwarks of our digital existence against impending threats.

Chapter 10. Challenges in Implementing Blockchain in IoT

Despite its promise to revolutionize IoT security, the integration of blockchain into IoT frameworks is riddled with a myriad of challenges that require careful consideration. A pragmatic and well-executed approach is requisite in overcoming the inevitable hurdles that dot the path to secure, efficient, and agile IoT operations bolstered by blockchain.

10.1. Understanding the Complexity of Integration

Integration of blockchain with IoT systems is not a direct plug and play. These are two distinct technologies developed for different purposes. IoT aims at interconnecting billions of devices for easy sharing and access of insights, while blockchain's design serves a facilitator of peer-to-peer transactions that bypass intermediation by banks.

Even with their respective strengths contributing to data security and connectivity, the integration of IoT and blockchain becomes a complex undertaking fraught with challenges. This is mainly because the blockchain was not initially intended for IoT, thus requires a significant overhaul of both technologies for a seamless integration. Accordingly, key considerations have to be made, such as changes to the IoT architecture, bandwidth needs, and data formats to ensure compatibility with blockchain protocols.

10.2. Scalability Concerns

Scalability is another concern that specialists grapple with when implementing blockchain in IoT. The purpose of IoT is to connect a vast number of devices, spanning from a household level to an industrial scale. It is estimated that by 2025, 75 billion IoT devices will be connected globally. This points to a stark reality; the anticipated hyper-connected world will be immense, thereby putting a colossal demand on the blockchain infrastructure employed.

Currently, blockchain technologies such as Bitcoin or Ethereum are facing issues in scalability. For instance, the Bitcoin blockchain can only process between three to seven transactions per second, and Ethereum can process approximately 15 transactions. This transaction capacity pales in comparison to the requirements of a global IoT network. Streamlining the efficiency of processing transactions in large volumes and at high speed is, therefore, a challenge that must be surmounted for effective delivery of IoT services on a blockchain platform.

10.3. Constraints in Processing and Storage Capacities

Blockchain's modus operandi involves detailed record keeping of every transaction that occurs on the platform. It is a characteristic feature that bolsters data security and promotes transparency. However, when viewed under the IoT lens, this detail-oriented approach presents a stumbling block as the number of devices accrue and interactions increase, accruing into a massive amount of data that has to be stored on the blockchain.

Given the decentralized nature of blockchain, every connected node in the network stores a replicated copy of the entire blockchain. With the number of IoT devices anticipated to be in billions, the storage requirements are enormous, thus stretching the limits of current capacities.

Simultaneously, the computational demands of processing blockchain transactions at scale are significant. Every entry into the blockchain requires validation by solving complex mathematical problems, a process that consumes substantial computational power. In an IoT-blockchain setup, meeting the computational needs given the huge volumes of data from IoT devices becomes a herculean task.

10.4. Energy Consumption and Sustainability Issues

The processing power required by blockchain to validate transactions infamously leads to high energy consumption. Bitcoin, for example, consumes more energy than some countries. The "Proof of Work" consensus methodology used by many blockchain implementations not only requires massive computational power to solve complex cryptographical tasks but these calculations also result in significant electrical power usage.

When this energy consumption factor comes into the fray with IoT, devices typically designed to be energy-efficient and to run on low power, it becomes another major challenge to effectively materialize blockchain-IoT integration. Striking a balance between ensuring security through blockchain and maintaining the energy efficiency of IoT devices presents a considerable task for technologists to grapple with.

10.5. Legal and Regulatory Ambiguity

Legal and regulatory frameworks concerning blockchain remain indistinct in many jurisdictions. Given blockchain's inception as a foundation for cryptocurrencies, many practices in security, data protection, and finance, among others, it has a state of regulatory ambiguity.

The integration of blockchain with IoT further compounds this challenge. IoT itself is wrestling with gaps in legal and regulatory frameworks on issues such as data protection, interoperability, and liability. As such, the amalgamation of IoT and blockchain intertwines the legislative and regulatory complexities of each, creating a quagmire that necessitates significant attention in order to develop standards and guidelines for implementing blockchain within IoT.

10.6. Building Trust and Acceptance

Beyond the technical and legal hurdles, the successful integration of blockchain in IoT also hinges on achieving user trust and societal acceptance. For the layperson, both technologies may be esoteric and evoke misperceptions or fears about potential misuse or failings. It is therefore critical to not only ensure blockchain and IoT integration delivers on its promises but also to effectively communicate these capabilities to potential users.

Realizing the full potential of both technologies in enhancing IoT security involves raising awareness on their mechanisms and addressing concerns about their use. This is an uphill task given the nascent state of both technologies and the various misconceptions associated with them.

In conclusion, pulling together the threads of IoT and blockchain holds considerable promise in advancing our digital lives securely. However, the implementation journey is a challenging endeavor that calls for robust strategies to counter multifaceted technical, regulatory, and social challenges. Only by conquering these difficulties can we truly secure our digital frontier using blockchain embedded IoT.

Chapter 11. Future Perspective: Advancements and Opportunities in Blockchain-IoT Integration

As we cast our eyes towards the horizon of technology, we see a future where every aspect of our digital life is intricately intertwined with smart devices in a rapidly expanding Internet of Things environment. In the midst of this impressive panorama, we find that Blockchain technology offers a robust solution to a major obstacle impeding this progress - ensuring the security of our proliferating digital footprints.

11.1. Potential of Blockchain-IoT Integration

The intersection of Blockchain and IoT holds immense potential. IoT devices, for their robust operation and efficient management, necessitate a secure protocol for data exchange. As per the current standard methodologies, these devices mostly rely on traditional data exchange protocols and centralized cloud storage - a model that holds latent vulnerabilities.

Blockchain, with its decentralized nature and robust cryptographic procedures, provides an impeccable solution. By integrating IoT devices with blockchain technology, data exchange can be made vastly more secure and efficient. Once an IoT device records data on the blockchain, it becomes almost tamper-proof and verifiable. For example, an IoT-enabled lock system can record every instance of its usage in a Blockchain, creating a timeline of events that cannot be altered retroactively.

In addition, Blockchain technology offers a unique advantage in IoT - peer to peer communication. IoT devices, when coupled with blockchain, can interact directly without the requirement of intermediaries, or middlemen. Data exchange becomes a direct process, making data transmission significantly faster and reducing the potential points of failure. .

11.2. The Shift Towards Decentralization

One of the prime reasons behind substantial growth in IoT is the integration of decentralized management tools. Centralized cloud storage systems, while powerful in their right, suffer from several problems. An example of such issues can be seen in terms of a single point of failure. If a central server fails, it can cause the entire network to falter.

Decentralized systems, on the other hand, are based on several nodes. If one node fails to work, it doesn't cripple the entire network. This resilience is especially critical in IoT networks, where network robustness can be a matter of utmost importance. Blockchain, as an inherently decentralized system, therefore provides a robust model for data management in IoT.

11.3. Use of Smart Contracts in IoT

Blockchain's "smart contracts" are another emergent area offering exciting potentials in the future of IoT. These contracts are a set of automated instructions that execute when predefined conditions are met.

In an IoT scenario, a smart contract on a blockchain could be used to automate complex processes. For instance, an IoT-equipped weather station could be programmed to place orders for specific services based on meteorological data, such as ordering salt trucks when the temperature drops below zero. This automation eradicates the manual inefficiencies thereby increasing productivity and potential for scale.

11.4. Challenges and the Road Ahead

Despite the immense potential, there are challenges that still need to be addressed before a full-scale integration of blockchain and IoT can be realized. The storage and computational requirement of blockchains can be substantial and may impact the performance of resource-constrained IoT devices. The speed of blockchain is another issue, as the technology isn't still capable of handling a significant number of transactions per second, which is required in a dense IoT network.

However, solutions to these challenges are actively being sought by several entities worldwide. Technologies like Sharding and the Lightning Network have shown promise in areas of transaction speed and storage, respectively.

The road to a fully integrated blockchain-IoT system might be long and full of challenges, but the advancements being made are offering up incredibly optimistic prospects. As we forge ahead, we can only anticipate a future where blockchain and IoT integration has radically altered the way we perceive data security and IoT.

This promising future, however, relies heavily upon ongoing research and development. As more organizations and governments awaken to the immense potential of Blockchain-IoT, we will undoubtedly see a surge in investment, regulation, and adoption of these technologies. This forward push opens up a plethora of opportunities for innovators, entrepreneurs and tech enthusiasts across the globe.

By staying informed and tuned in to these developments, we are not merely passive observers of the future but active participants, shaping the course of digital evolution. This exciting journey of discovery continually pushes the envelope on what's possible, pushing us closer to a future where technology is seamlessly ingrained into every facet of our lives, unobtrusively serving us and preserving our digital identities with unmatched integrity and resilience.